Options Trading

An Introduction for Beginners

By

John Gibson

Copyright 2018 by John Gibson - All rights reserved.

The following book is reproduced below with the goal of providing information that is as accurate and reliable as possible. Regardless, purchasing this book can be seen as consent to the fact that both the publisher and the author of this book are in no way experts on the topics discussed within and that any recommendations or suggestions that are made herein are for entertainment purposes only. Professionals should be consulted as needed prior to undertaking any of the action endorsed herein.

This declaration is deemed fair and valid by both the American Bar Association and the Committee of Publishers Association and is legally binding throughout the United States.

Furthermore, the transmission, duplication or reproduction of any of the following work including specific information will be considered an illegal act irrespective of if it is done electronically or in print. This extends to creating a secondary or tertiary copy of the work or a recorded copy and is only allowed with express written consent from the Publisher. All additional right reserved.

The information in the following pages is broadly considered to be a truthful and accurate account of facts and as such any inattention, use or misuse of the information in question by the reader will render any resulting actions solely under their purview. There are no scenarios in which the publisher or the original author of this work can be in any fashion deemed liable for any hardship or damages that may befall them after undertaking information described herein.

Additionally, the information in the following pages is intended only for informational purposes and should thus be thought of as universal. As befitting its nature, it is presented without assurance regarding its prolonged validity or interim quality. Trademarks that are mentioned are done without written consent and can in no way be considered an endorsement from the trademark holder.

Table of Contents

Introduction 4

Chapter 1: Options and Their Options..7

Chapter 2: The Foundation- Your Brokerage Account and Platform..18

Chapter 3: Risk Profile Charts 24

Chapter 4: Buying Calls and Puts 33

Chapter 5: Buying Calls and Puts- Part 2 49

Chapter 6: Option Strategy #1 68

Chapter 7: Option Strategy #2 78

Chapter 8: Putting it All Together 91

Introduction

The financial markets brim with potential wealth for all its participants. On a large scale, they are inherently fair and its only those with the correct skills and strategies that survive and thrive. The markets do not care about things such as your feelings, your background, your current financial situation or anything else. All that matters is that you understand its mechanics and implement correct strategies to exploit situations that arise within them. Over the years, the nature of the market has changed but the spirit of it has remained the same, that is, one of ambition, innovation and simplicity in the face of potential complexity.

The markets these days give you a number of options to develop and execute your strategy. Be it forex or stocks or bonds, the number of choices are endless. The greatest of these opportunities is perhaps the derivatives market. Derivatives have exploded in number over the years but their very essence is one of maximizing reward and minimizing risk. Some derivatives have complex mathematical structures and yet others have what may seem ridiculous stipulations built into them (for example weather related structured products). Furthermore, the naming convention of these derivatives is more than enough to scare away any beginner and creates the illusion that only professionals ought to be involved in such things and that the beginner is best served sitting quietly at home playing with her marbles.

While it is true that the complexity of some derivatives puts them out of the reach of your average trader, the idea that they can only be understood by professionals or that it takes some God like intelligence to understand is one of the many lies Wall Street and the other financial houses have been feeding you to justify their own existence. In reality, derivatives can be understood through a simple learning process and once you grasp the basics, you will fully be able to exploit these instruments.

The only derivatives you need to understand to make money in the markets are futures and options. This series of books will concern itself with options, specifically vanilla options. Don't let the term vanilla intimidate your or imply to you that this is something of a kindergarten level. The reality is that such options are simple and their full power lies in their simplicity. Those who make a living by selling complex things are doing so to simply justify their own intellect and existence to themselves. You simply do not need to understand or even know of complex derivatives to succeed. If you're still not convinced, let me assure you, the vast majority of hedge funds employ strategies which use simple options. The ones which use complex derivatives are the ones ones you read about in the paper once they go under.

In this book, I will introduce you, the beginner, to the basics of an option, the types of options and strategies you can use. Interspersed between all this is my own experience and insight I've gained over the years as a professional trader which I'm positive you'll find invaluable.

So enough of the introduction, let's now step forth in to the exciting world of options!

Chapter 1: Options and Their Options

Options present the knowledgeable trader and indeed, investor, with opportunities to both diversify, speculate and also reduce the risk of their portfolios. This book is of course directed towards traders and speculators so investors will need to look elsewhere for portfolio hedging strategies. I'm merely mentioning it to illustrate the versatility of these financial instruments. Options are a type of instrument known as derivatives. Now, since the market crash of 2008, derivatives have become a curse word of sorts and all sorts of world ending powers have been granted them by the public. Nothing is further from the truth. The reality is the instruments by themselves have little power. It is the trader who speculates in them who needs to prepare for all possibilities and cover her downside risk. Just as how a beginner trader can lose everything through improper risk management so can a professional. The rules remain the same, you see, no matter the level at which you operate.

I do not wish to present options as something which will solve all your trading woes however. You still need to prepare and understand how they work inside out. If you already have a broker, you will have noticed the disclaimer they place before every option: *"Losses may exceed deposits. Trade with risk capital only"*. This is due to the nature of the instruments themselves but you shouldn't assume because of this that options are better suited for professionals. The way I'd put it is that just like every other financial instrument, options are suited for those willing to put in the work and preparation to understand them and for those who understand risk management.

Options offer a great deal of versatility wen used correctly but before getting into all that, let's take a step back and define what a derivative is first off all: A derivative is a financial instrument whose value is derived from some other instrument. For example: ketchup is a derivative of tomatoes. The worse the tomatoes, the worse the ketchup. Similarly, your results are a derivative of your process. The worse your process, the worse your results. Options are merely one type of derivative instrument. They can be used and tailored to fit your own trading style. Indeed, many traders who struggle with stocks tend to relish options because of the different nature of the market. In my experience, once traders reach a certain level of proficiency with the stock market, the options market always seems more attractive to them.

An option itself can be defined as such: An options gives the holder the right, but not the obligation, to buy or sell the underlying security/instrument. In plain English, if you hold an option, it gives you the right to buy or sell the stock/underlying instrument it is derived from. But you don't *have* to do so. You merely have the "option" to do so. Whoever sold you the option, however, has to deliver the underlying instrument to you, should you choose to exercise your option. In short, if you exercise your option, the seller has an obligation to deliver as per the terms of the option. We'll be looking at two kinds of options throughout this book and both types of options have two components: an agreed upon price and an agreement to deliver within a certain period or a specific date.

The 2 kinds of options we'll be looking at here are calls and puts. A call option gives you the right but not the obligation to buy the underlying at a certain price either within a certain time period or on a particular date. You may think of this via the following example: Let's say you're in the market for a house. However, for some reason you don't trust the builder and wish to purchase only if they install 4 bathrooms as per your specifications (unrealistic I know, but this is an example after all). Now, if the developer offered you a contract whereby you paid a small fraction of the cost of the house and the developer is obliged to build the 4 bathrooms as per your specs within one month or else you do not buy the house, that would seem like a good solution to your issue wouldn't it? Well, that's what a call option is. If you like stock XYZ and think that it will double in price within the next month, you can buy a call option which expires within a month. You pay a fraction of the cost of the amount you would have had to pay if you bought the stock and you get the right to buy it at any time over the next month. If the stock does go up, you can either sell your call option or you can exercise your right to purchase the stock. Similarly, a put option gives you the right to sell the underlying at an agreed upon price within a defined time period or on a particular date.

Now you must be wondering what the "sell within a defined time period or particular date" is about. Well, this is essentially the difference between a European and an American option. A European option can only be exercised on a particular date. At no other point can it be exercised by the purchaser. It can be traded of course but simply not exercised. An American option on the other hand can be exercised at any date or time prior to its expiry. It you purchase an American option which expires in a month's time, you can exercise it at any time between now and a month. Due to this additional flexibility, American options trade at a slight premium or extra charge compared to European options. Just to clarify, American and European options are available on any instrument you choose, irrespective of whether the underlying is of European or American origin. The terms "American" and "European" are merely used as a classification and do not denote the origin of the underlying.

Another aspect of options you must understand is the strike price. The strike price is simply the price at which the option becomes beneficial to exercise. So for example, an American call option on say, IBM, with a strike price of $65 and an expiry of one month from today is just a contract that gives you the right to buy IBM at $65 at any time within a month (since its an American option). How many shares of IBM can you buy? Well that's what the contract size is. Contract sizes vary depending on instruments and markets but generally they are in multiples of 100. Similarly, a European put option on IBM with a contract size of 100, strike price of $40 and an expiry date of 1/5/2018 gives you the right but not the obligation to sell 100 shares of IBM only on 1/5/2018 (since its a European option) and not at any time else.

Some other points I wish to point out are that since you have no obligation to exercise the option you're free to do nothing as the option expires. Your loss is limited to the price you paid for the option itself. Therefore your loss is limited while your upside is unlimited if your plan works out. This brings me to the term "in the money". No doubt you will have seen this on most financial broadcasts which list market action. An "in the money" option is one where the underlying is on the right side of the strike price. That is, if the market price is greater than the strike price of a call option, it is in the money. If it is greater than the strike price of a put option, it is not in the money. It is only in the the money when the market price is lower than the strike price of the put.

Essentially, a call option is taking a long position in the market. You buy calls when you're of the belief that the market will rise. After all this is how call holders make money. For example, using the previous IBM situation, lets say the price of IBM today is $40. You believe it will trade at $80 within a month. Therefore, you buy a call option which expires in a month with a strike price of 65$. If IBM trades above $65 within the option expiry date, you have a profit (less what you paid for the call). If it trades at 65 or below, you have a loss that is limited to the price you paid for the call. Therefore, you make money only when the price rises, which is equivalent to a buy or long position. Similarly, buying a put is equivalent to shorting the market but with far less risk than a naked short. You will make a profit depending on how far below the strike price the market price is less the cost of the put. If the market is still trading above the strike price on the expiration date, your loss is limited to the price of the put.

The price of an option fluctuates based on the underlying market price and the volatility of the underlying instrument. The price is determined using the Black-Scholes formula which takes these underlying factors into account. This formula was developed by American economists, Fischer Black and Myron Scholes along with Robert C. Merton (not to be confused with his illustrious father, the psychologist, Robert K. Merton). They were awarded the Nobel prize in 1997 for their efforts. Their formula is, however, based on an economic model and like all economic models, relies on a set of assumptions which aren't always true. Thus, the pricing of options isn't an exact science but is something which follows a least worst method principle. My reasoning behind choosing the words "least worst" as opposed to "the best we currently have" is something beyond the scope of this book and indeed, this topic itself. If you are interested in this however, I highly recommend reading *When Genius Failed* by Roger Lowenstein or *The Big Short* by Michael Lewis.

The price of an option is subject to speculative forces just like its underlying instrument. Generally as the market price approaches the strike price of an option, its value increases and so does its price. In other words a call option with a strike price of 65 is far more valuable when the underlying market price is 70 as opposed to an underlying market price of 40. Similarly a put option increases in price as underlying market price decreases towards the strike price and goes below it. Option pricing is an intensely mathematical and theoretical subject which doesn't really give any major advantage while speculating. The only possible strategy you can exploit by digging into the Black-Scholes equation is by realizing its limitations. For example, the theorem always undervalues extreme price valuations or volatility that is beyond expected values. Many investors take advantage of this inefficiency by betting on special situations like bankruptcy or court rulings in certain stocks whereby a single event can cause a major movement in the underlying price. Since this major movement will be larger than historic volatility level, the options are consequently under priced and can provide excellent profits. This is not a strategy I'll be exploring here since quite frankly, there are easier ways to make money and secondly, everyone knows this by now and the inefficiency isn't as great as it used to be.

A simpler and more understanding of option pricing is as follows. The price of an option, called the premium, is made of two parts. The intrinsic value and the time value. The intrinsic value is simply the difference between the market price and the strike price. For a call option, the market price is subtracted from the strike price (IV= Market price- Strike price) and for a put its the other way round (IV=Strike Price-Market price). The time value has a quantitative and qualitative aspect to it. Qualitatively speaking, the time value is simply the price you're willing to pay to give the option time to work out. For example, if you own a put with a strike price of 20 and the current market price is 30, the probability of the option going below your strike price is a function of the time left till expiry. In other words, if there's a month left, you;d be willing to pay more for that option as opposed to a scenario where there's a week left. Quantitatively, this amount is merely the premium (that is, price of the option) minus the intrinsic value. This formula is merely mathematical but it gives us a number to look at and aids in comparison.

To sum up, the following factors affect the option premium:

- Underlying market price
- Strike price
- The volatility of the instrument underlying

The benefits of trading options are plenty but can essentially be boiled down to: leverage. Options allow you to get in on the action for a far lesser price than if you bought/sold the underlying stocks and allow you to access the same reward you would have had if you bought/sold the stock. Thus, you have freedom to allocate more capital to situations you think are interesting. There are some downsides to trading options though. The leverage acts as a double edged sword an can often magnify losses if you don't know what you're doing. Options trading is also slightly more complex compared to trading other assets and those without a mathematical bent might find this unsuitable.

All in all though, if you can stomach the mathematical and graphical demands options trading places on you, you'll find them quite rewarding and profitable than plain vanilla stock trading strategies.

Chapter 2: The Foundation- Your Brokerage Account and Platform

Before we get to the meaty bits about strategies and such its important to go over the process over choosing a broker and platform for trading options. The reason is that options trading commission structures are a bit more complex than your average stock brokerage not to mention the fact that ease of usage and execution is of even more essence here. There are a number of trading platforms available, both online and offline (although who would choose a purely offline system is beyond me). This chapter will give you some quick and easy ways to evaluate your platform and enable you to make the best decision. Also, it pays to remember that choosing a platform isn't a life or death issue. You can always open another account.

Before even opening an account I highly recommend you take a look at your capitalization level. This is true of any form of trading, in that you should only be trading money you can afford to lose, but doubly so in the case of options. I suggest the following criteria at a minimum:

- Do you have a steady source of income with which you can

maintain your current standards for the next year at least? In other words, is there any chance of disruption to that income?

- Have you made some money trading stocks previously? Even if you broke even trading stocks, that's great.

- Do you have adequate savings lined up? Have you resolved to yourself and your partner/spouse that under no circumstances will you be touching this money?

- Do you have at least 5,000 USD in capital to trade options?

If you answered "no" to any of the above, then I recommend not trading options. The only exception is point 2 regarding trading stocks. While its not completely necessary, some market knowledge should be there for you to understand options, it just makes your journey easier.

In the United States, all brokers have 5 levels of options trading available to customers. These levels determine what sort of strategies you're allowed to employ. For example, you can employ basic call and put strategies and even covered call strategies on the basic levels and your broker will not require you deposit any amount as a minimum balance prior to doing so. However if you choose to write uncovered puts, this is something only level 5 traders are allowed to execute and you will be required to post a minimum balance with the broker. Internationally, the standards are the same in developed markets like Europe and Australia. The Asian markets, except Japan, are the wild west as far as regulation is concerned and while it is possible to run any strategy you like out there, I highly recommend being sensible at the start and only executing simple, easy to understand strategies.

The best way to discover which broker is right for you is to ideally be able to demo trade their platform first and then make an informed decision. Unlike the forex market though, options brokers very rarely agree to such terms. Here's a little known fact though that you won't read anywhere else. Using this, you can get access to not just one but three options platforms completely free of charge via a demo account. Simply go to the CBOE website (that's the Chicago Board Option Exchange) and register there to get free access to three options trading platforms. Take them out for a spin as long as you want!

All brokers offer the platforms free of charge. The catch is they make their money via commissions. While the rates are quite competitive, it still pays to compare and check everyone out. If you have a large enough account size (if you have to ask what that threshold is, your account probably isn't large enough) you can always negotiate with a broker. The other confusing fact about trading options are the various structures that different brokers use. For example, some brokers charge a flat fee irrespective of the number of contracts you purchase, others charge a fixed rate per contract while others offer hybrid structures whereby you pay a fixed fee plus a rate per contract. While the overall rates you pay will be somewhat close to each other, irrespective of the structure, you need to obviously pick the lowest cost structure nonetheless. The best way to evaluate this is to look at it in terms of your trading strategy.

A lot of options strategies require you to adjust your position size as the trade matures. So this involves either increasing or reducing your position size. Under such a strategy, the first structure illustrated in the previous example would be extremely expensive since you'll be paying the same rate for, say 20 options (which could be your initial position) as well as for 5 options (which could be your position adjustment). In such a scenario a fixed rate per contract structure would serve you best. Some strategies are designed to simply take advantage of the movement of the underlying stock and do not call for any adjustments. Given this scenario, a commission structure like the first one would make the most sense. As you can see, its all about your strategy.

There are some brokers out there, and this is mostly true of the international scene, who will offer you bonuses and other perks on signing up. While my general advice is to stay away form these types of brokers, it pays to evaluate what their offer is. If the introductory rate is quite low but the usual rate is high for your strategy then it doesn't make sense to sign up. Also, in this book, I will not be covering binary options since that is something we'll look at in a later book in this series.

Options quotes can be be quite complicated to read at first but are simple to understand when broken down. As an example consider the following quote: AAPL140120P005500000. At first glance it looks like a piece of computer code which has broken out by mistake. The way you read this quote is by understanding that all the information regarding the option is mentioned right there within it.

AAPL= Apple. This is the stock ticker

140120= 14/01/20. Expiration date is 14th of January 2020

P= Put. This is a put option. A call will have a C in it.

005500000= 550. This option is priced at $550.

This is the standard naming procedure across all developed markets. You may find a few tiny differences but overall this convention holds.

So now that we've covered the brokers, let's dive into risk profile diagrams which will help you understand strategy evaluation a lot better.

Chapter 3: Risk Profile Charts

Risk profile charts are somewhat unique to the world of options trading since this arena involves a lot of mathematical calculations. By placing the trade on a graphical medium, we can understand the risk we're undertaking better. This is the basis on which we will build out strategies and evaluate them. There are 4 steps to creating a risk profile chart.

1. First we draw a horizontal axis representing the price of the underlying stock.

2. Second, we draw a vertical line and label it as profit/loss. This axis will signify our P/L for the position per share.

3. Third, we draw our breakeven line. This is in the middle of the Y axis and we annotate this with a 0 on the Y/vertical axis.

4. Lastly, we create the risk profile. This depends on the strategy we're employing. Let's now look at a few basic strategies operations and their risk profiles.

When we buy a stock, the trade has a certain risk profile. This can be represented by the following diagram.

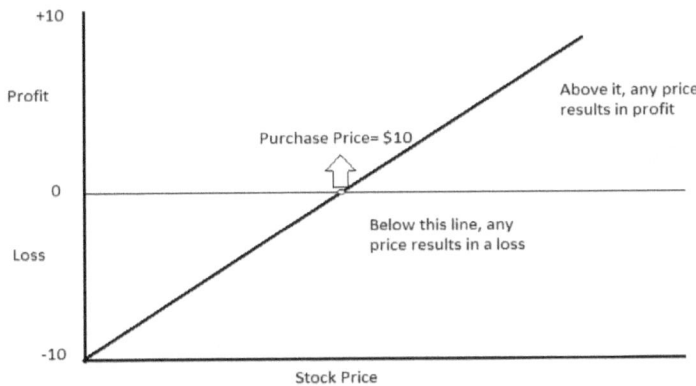

We buy a share of stock for 10$ and thus this is our break even level. If the price of the stock is 10, your P/L will be 0. This is represented by the horizontal break even line on the chart. If the price is 20 (or increases by +10), your profit increases proportionately to 10$. Similarly, if the price goes to 0 (or decreases by -10), your loss increases proportionately to -10$. Hence, your P/L increases or decreases proportionately to the underlying price and thus the curve we get is a 45 degree line with a positive slope.

What does shorting a stock look like? Well, if we shorted it at 10$ and the price decreased by 10$, we would have 10$ in profit.

If the price increases by 10$ we will have a loss of 10$. This creates the risk profile curve as below.

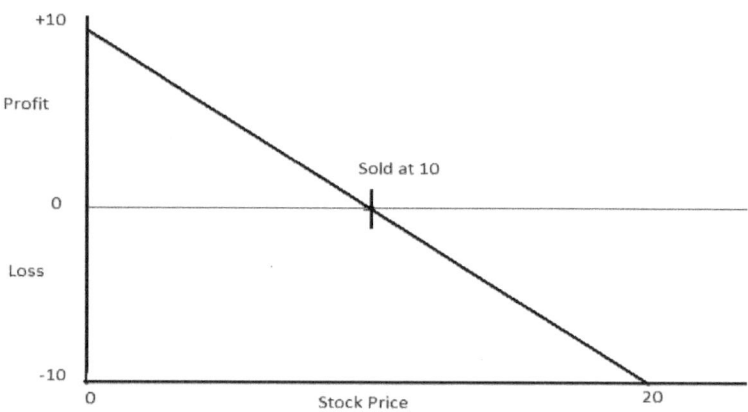

What this curve communicates is that the lower our stock price is, the greater our profit. The higher the price goes, the lower our profit is. This curve also highlights the risk of shorting since as you can see, the downside is unlimited since the stock price can rise infinitely. Contrast this to the previous graph and you'll see the downside is limited since the lowest any price can go to is 0.

Now when you purchase an option, you need to pay the premium, or cost of the option. What would the risk curves for a call and a put look like?

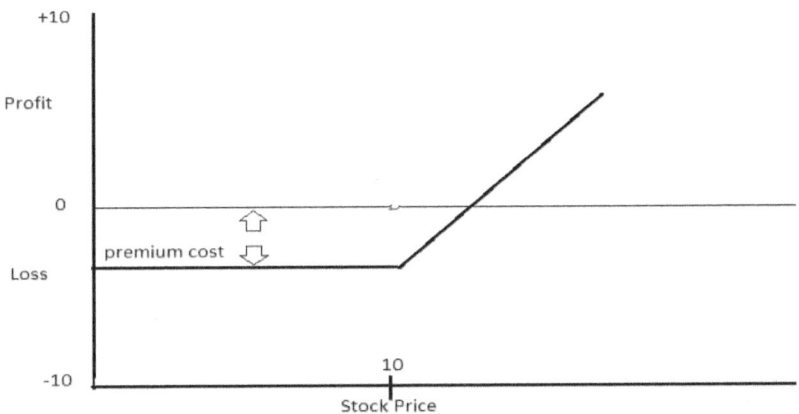

The above risk profile is that of a call. Remember a call is the right to buy a stock at a strike price. Assuming the strike price here is 10, the call is essentially worthless to us as long as the price is below 10. Since we paid a premium to purchase the call, our maximum possible loss on this trade is the premium amount. This is why our risk curve starts below 0. The option is valuable only once price crosses the strike price and our trade moves into greater profit as the price increases.

Similarly a put has a premium that needs to be paid upon purchase. The put is valuable only when the underlying price is below the strike price. Our maximum reward is achieved when the price of the underlying stock reaches 0. As long as the price is above the strike price, our maximum possible loss is capped at the amount which we paid for the premium. Using this information, go ahead and try to draw a risk curve for a put. Check the next diagram to see if you were correct.

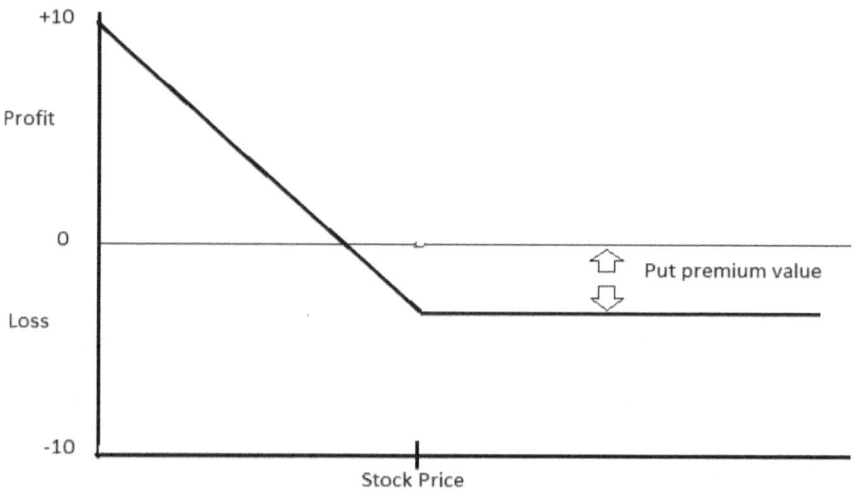

This is a great moment to illustrate the benefits of using options. Compare the risk curves of the short trade and the put. You'll notice the put has the same reward profile of the short but while the short has an unlimited downside, the put caps it drastically to the value of the put option premium. There is not better way to describe the benefits of options than this.

Since this is a book for beginners, I'm not covering the aspects of selling calls and puts. Apart from adding complexity, this merely exposes beginners to strategies which require excellent risk management which you will probably not have at this stage. For the sake of completeness however, I am listing the risk profiles of a call sell and a put sell. Try to draw them yourself before looking at the charts. By selling a call, I am obligated to sell the underlying stock to the buyer and by selling a put I'm obligated to buy the underlying stock from the buyer. In the case of the call, my profit is the value of the option premium the buyer pays me as long as the price remains under the striker price and my loss is unlimited once the price is greater than the strike price. Reason it similarly for the put and compare your efforts to the charts.

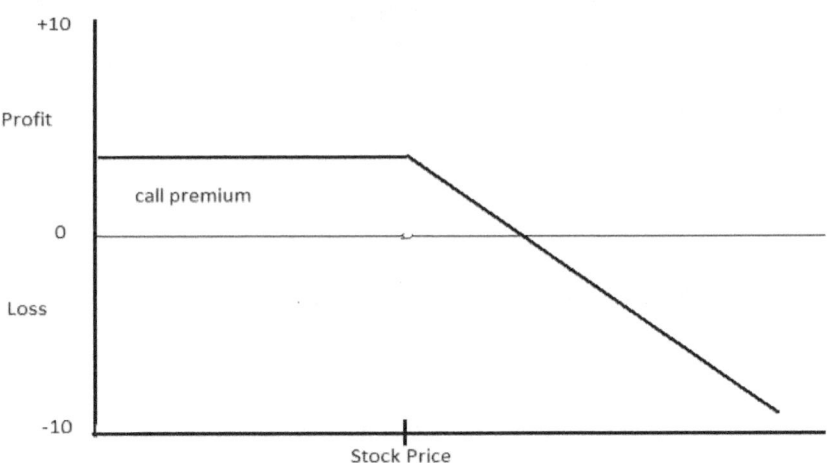

The above is a risk profile of a call sell.

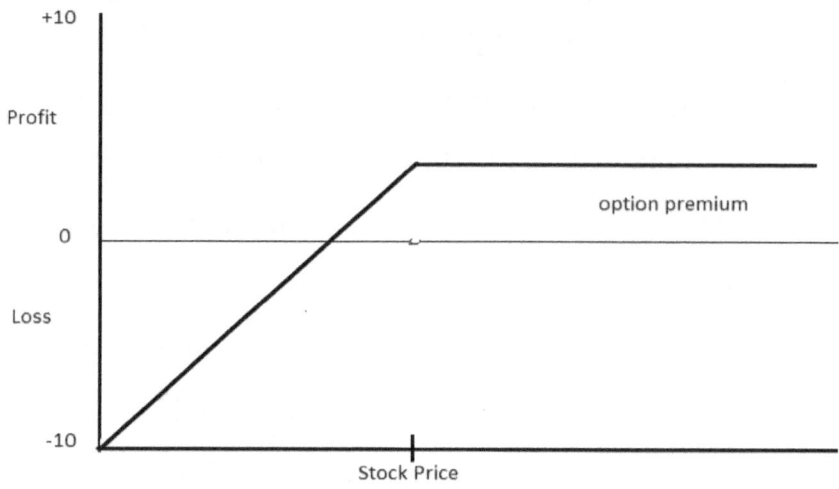

The above is the profile of a put sell. My profit is limited to the premium as long as the stock price is above the strike price. Once it dives below the strike price, my loss is limited to how far it has to go to 0.

We will now briefly look at an intermediate concept which I believe a beginner should know about before diving into strategies. This is the concept of the hedge ratio or delta for short. Delta is one of the many greeks you'll meet when trading options so you might as well start now. Delta is best illustrated using an example. In this example I'll be assuming the time value of an option doesn't change for simplicity's sake. Suppose we buy a put with a strike price of 25 and the underlying stock price is 30. Lets say the premium we pay is 1$ which is entirely the time premium since the intrinsic value is 0 (remember for a put intrinsic value= strike price- stock price).

Now if the stock price goes to 20, and assuming the time value remains the same, the intrinsic value of the put is now 5 (i.e 25-20). The option price is now 6 (5 intrinsic+ 1 Time). This represents an increase of 500% (from 1 to 6) while the stock price has decreased only 33% (from 30 to 20). The option is clearly more leveraged and gives up far greater profits compared to the underlying stock. However, this sort of leverage goes both ways. The delta measures the ratio between the change in option price and the change in the underlying price. A good strategy always looks to minimize the delta since while leverage gives us great profits, it is the cause of even greater losses if risk is not managed correctly.

This finishes our look at options basics. We're now ready to look at some strategies you can use immediately to make money. Take some time to understand the basics especially the risk profiles before moving on. The better your understanding, the easier it will be for you to understand the upcoming material.

Chapter 4: Buying Calls and Puts

The simplest strategy we'll be looking at first is simply buying calls. Much like how you purchase stock in anticipation of an upward move, you enter a long position on the option instead of purchasing the stock. The advantages of this strategy is the lower margin requirements and a potentially larger reward depending on the underlying stock's volatility. The lower margin required means you can take a greater number of positions than you usually would and this gives you a greater number of opportunities for your strategy to work. The question is: What is your strategy?

There are many technical indicators out there based on which you can design a strategy. However, not all of them work over long periods simply because they're either too simplistic or too mechanical. The real solution to building a system is to have discretionary elements to it which therefore cannot be copied by anyone else. Over the next 2 chapters I'll be highlighting the best indicators for you to use and also how you can use them within a system. First off we look at the Ichimoku cloud and how you can use it to predict both bullish and bearish movements in a stock or any instrument.

IKH or Ichimoku for short looks like an extremely complicated indicator at first glance. The average Ichimoku chart contains 5 lines which seem to go all over the place. However, on closer examination, you will find that the Ichimoku cloud is an elegant and concise indicator wrapping all sorts of market information into one chart. The name itself translates from Japanese as "one look equilibrium chart". While that translation doesn't alleviate the confusion as to what this is, it actually does describe an Ichimoku chart very well.

Briefly, the objective of the Ichimoku cloud is to give the trader an instant snapshot of the market trend, support and resistance levels, momentum of the current trend and entry and exit signals. As you can imagine that's a lot of information crammed into a few lines and thus on the surface, makes Ichimoku seem confusing. This indicator works best on Japanese stocks and Yen pairs in forex. This is mainly due to the fact that the majority of traders in Asian markets use this indicator thus making it more efficient. The "cloud" refers to all the lines within an Ichimoku chart and is comprised of the following lines:

- Kijun Sen- Also referred to as the standard line or base line. The usual setting for this line is 26. This translates, on a daily chart, as the midpoint of the high-low range over a period of 26 days. The calculation is shown below:

Base line= (26 period high+ 26 period low)/2

- Tenkan Sen- Also referred to as the conversion line. This line is the midpoint of the 9 day high-low range. So on a daily chart, its the midpoint of the 9 days high-low average. The calculation is as below:

Conversion Line= (9 period high+9 period low)/2

- Chikou Span- This is a line which tracks the bar close but is plotted 26 bars in the past. So on a chart, the current position of this line indicates the bar close 26 bars ago.

- Senkou Span A- Also referred to as the Leading Span A, this line forms one of the 2 lines which make up the cloud boundaries. The value is the midpoint between the conversion line and base line. This is plotted 26 periods ahead.vThe calculation is as below:

Leading Span A= (conversion line+ base line)/2

- Senkou Span B- Also referred to as Leading Span B, this is the other line which forms the Ichimoku cloud. This line is the average of the 52 period high and low and is plotted 26 periods into the future. The calculation is as below:

Leading Span B= (52 period high+ 52 period low)/2

Before we begin a dive into the specifics of this indicator please note, I'll be using the English names for these lines. Also, if you observe the charts to follow you will notice the following properties which hold true across all instruments;

- The Conversion line is usually the fastest and follows price the most closely. This stands to reason since its the 9 day average.
- The Base line, which is effectively a 26 day moving average is slower than the conversion line but tracks price decently as well.

The chart on the next page illustrates the various lines in play. The cloud itself is denoted with solid black color when the Leading Span A is <u>above</u> Leading Span B and as vertical stripes when Leading Span A is <u>below</u> Leading Span B. The base line and conversion line are presented as thick lines and the Chikou Span as the dotted line.

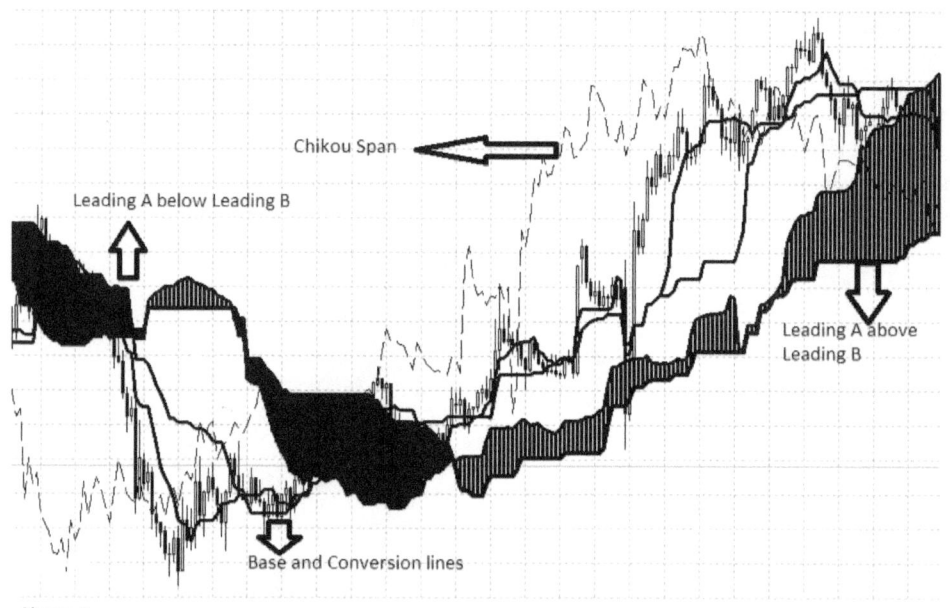

Figure 4

The Leading Span A and B are sometimes referred to as the Up Kumo and Down Kumo in certain charting software.

Some general trend conclusions can be drawn from a chart with the cloud on it. Prices are considered to be in an uptrend when above the cloud, downtrend when below it and in a range when within it. Further, the uptrend is strengthened when Leading Span A is above Span B, that is, the cloud is filled with vertical stripes as per the previous chart, and the downtrend is strengthened when Span A is below Span B, or the cloud is fully colored as per the previous chart.

The cloud also offers us a support/resistance level as per current price action but also in the future. This is because the entire cloud is plotted forward 26 days and can give us a good glimpse of probable future price action. In general it is important to remember that we ought to favor signals which are in line with the larger trend. That is, we prefer bullish signals when the price is above the cloud and the cloud is filled with stripes (that is, leading span A is above B) and bearish signals when price is below the cloud and is solid in color (that is A is below B). Any counter signals such as a bullish signal when price is below the cloud or span A is below B, is considered weak and I recommend beginners stay away from such signals.

This indicator throws up a variety of signals so let us now look at each one of them in greater detail.

Price/Cloud Crossover Signals

The position of price above or below the cloud, as previously mentioned, indicates or reinforces an existing bullish or bearish trend. Thus it stands to reason that a price crossover of the cloud indicates a trend change and is a reliable entry signal for us.

The direction is further enforced due to the cloud being plotted 26 period in the future.

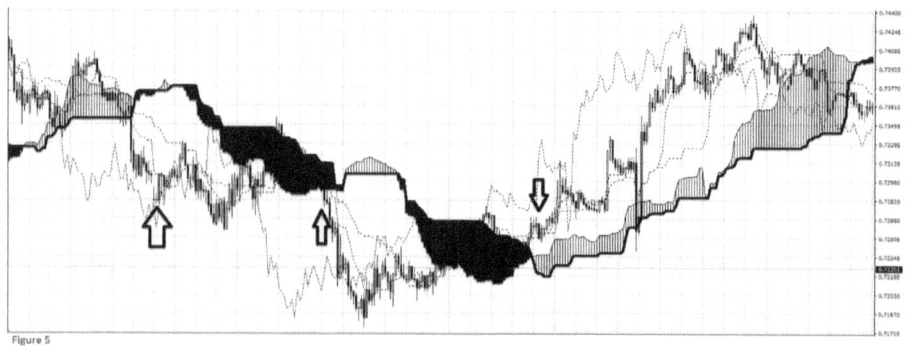
Figure 5

Figure 5 above illustrates how effective the crossover strategy is. The above chart of the NZD/USD fx pair is of the 60 minute timeframe. Notice how when price has multiple closes below the cloud and when the cloud is colored solid, that is, span B is above A, price tends to continue downwards for a while. The same pattern repeats itself on the bullish side as we move towards the right of the chart.

There isn't any fixed rule about how to enter in such situations. If you're following a moving average crossover strategy, then you can use similar entry rules as that. I recommend entering only when price has printed a few bars closing below or above the cloud. A conservative stop placement would be past the top of the Span B in bearish cases and below Span B in bullish cases. You will need to play around with this to see which fits you best since every trader has a different definition of risk. Experiment with it and implement that strategy which makes you the most money on paper.

Base and Conversion line crossovers

We saw earlier how these two lines are essentially the 9 day and 26 day moving averages of price. The difference between a traditional, western moving average and these lines though is that, the base and conversion lines are comprised of the mid point of prices as opposed to the close. Additionally, their effectiveness is enhanced when used in conjunction with the cloud and thus, gives rise to more accurate entries.

The crossover system works much the same as a moving average crossover but in this case we start with the cloud first. Price being above or below the cloud is what gives us our first read with regards to current price trend. Once this is has been established we then look at the base and conversion lines to spot any crossovers occurring. If a crossover does happen, for example, the conversion line, which is faster, crosses the base line, which is slower, we can conclude that this is a bullish signal. The relevance of this crossover though needs to be cross checked with the position of price relative to the cloud. If, in this example, price is below the cloud, and thus bearish, the signal really isn't of any relevance at the moment. We would simply sit tight and wait to see if price jumps above the cloud in which case we'd look for an entry, assuming the conversion line is still above the base line. Similarly, we would look for short entries where once the conversion line dips below the base line, we would confirm the validity using the cloud and then enter or sit tight as appropriate.

This double confirmation is what sets the crossover within the Ichimoku system apart from the traditional moving average crossover. Since we doubly confirm the trend direction prior to entry, there is a lesser chance of our signal being incorrect. That's not to say an incorrect signal won't occur, just that the cloud makes it less probable.

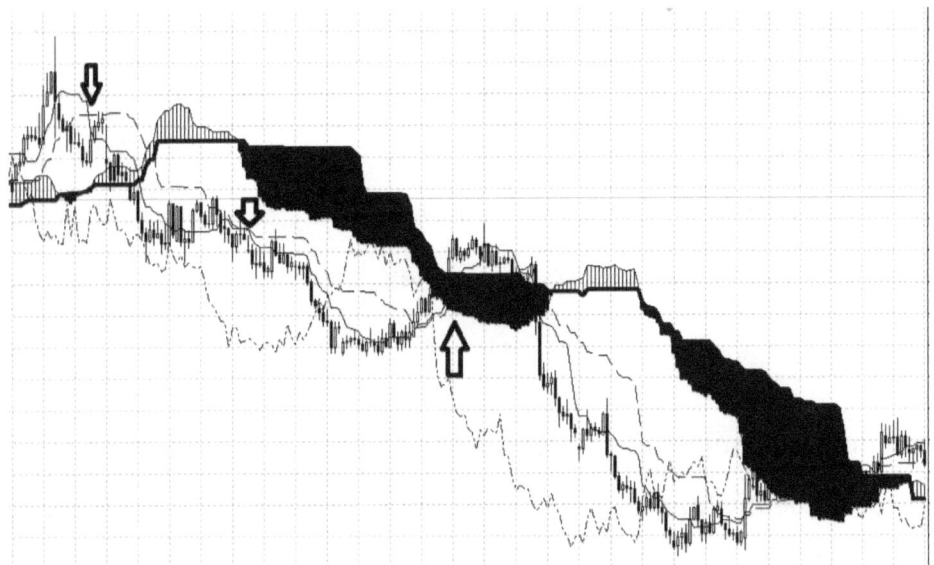
Figure 6: The Conversion line is solid and the base line is dashed with large components.

In figure 6, we see this system in action in a bear trend. At the first arrow, we see the conversion line dip below the base line but price remains firmly above the cloud. Thus for now we sit tight and wait for further developments. Price soon dips below the cloud and the conversion line is still below the base line, therefore this gives us an opportunity to enter short. Notice the two subsequent arrows. The smaller, downward pointing arrow indicates an area where the conversion line momentarily crosses over the base line. However, look at where price is relative to the cloud. This is thus an invalid bullish signal. The final, larger, upward pointing arrow shows us how no system is infallible.

Here after the conversion line crosses over the base line, price briefly goes over the cloud and this would have been a valid bullish signal. If we were to use the crossover system then this would have resulted in a loss. There is a way to avoid such false signals though as we will see in the next section.

For now it is important to remember the order in which the chart needs to be evaluated. The cloud comes first and then we look at the base and conversion lines to check for any signal or remain on the alert for one. As you can see from the above image, this system works as both a trend continuation and reversal signal which makes it pretty unique among technical indicators. The cloud also helps us avoid false signals as detailed previously thus increasing our accuracy rate. There is one more method the cloud gives us to increase our accuracy rate though. This involves the underrated and thus far largely unmentioned Chikou Span.

Using the Chikou Span

Thus far we haven't really looked too much at the Chikou Span. Indeed, I haven't even referred to it by its English name, the lagging line. As defined previously, this line is merely the closing price shifted 26 periods behind. There are 2 ways in which the lagging line can be used.

The first is to compare the line to the price itself and ascertain its position. Common wisdom is that if price is above the lagging line then we can confirm price is in a bull trend. Similarly, if price is below the lagging line then we're in a bear trend. While there are traders out there who use this effectively, in my opinion, this is not the most effective way of using this line. The reason is that by doing so, we're merely relegating this line into a quasi-moving average crossover type system. Just because price is above or below the level it was 26 periods ago doesn't make for a very useful entry indicator. As such, if you wish to figure out the direction of trend, the cloud itself is a much better indicator given the way its calculated.

The more effective usage of the lagging line is to compare its position with the cloud instead of the current price. The cloud gives us a better idea of the general trend and takes into account a larger number of price bars (obviously compared to just the current price). Thus the positioning of the lagging line with respect to the cloud gives us an additional layer of confirmation prior to our entries. In figure 6 previously, we saw how the last arrow indicated a loss when following the basic crossover system. Looking at that picture again, we can see that at the time the signal was generated, the lagging line was firmly below the cloud 26 bars before the arrow. This is a bit hard to visualize so I've put the same chart below this time indicating the level of the lagging line 26 periods behind the level where the signal was generated. If you were trading this live, you would have seen the lagging line end at the point marked by the circle.

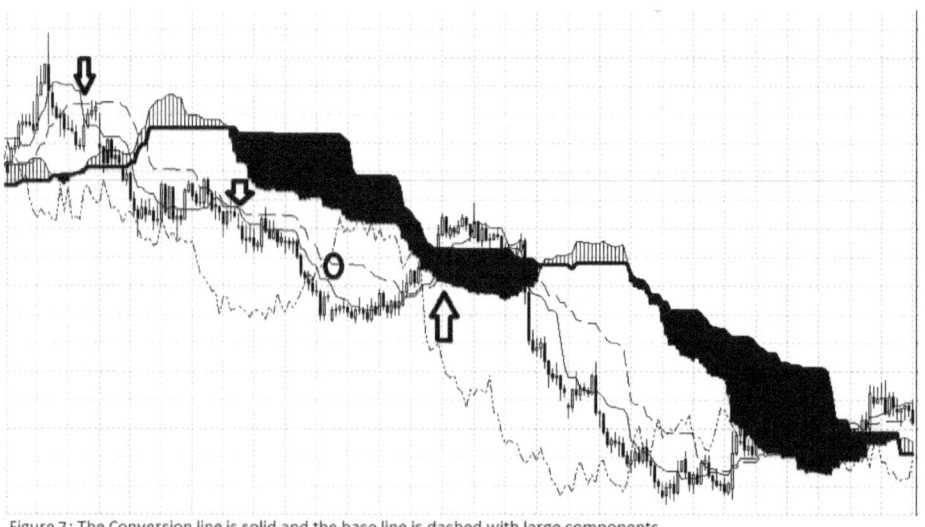

Figure 7: The Conversion line is solid and the base line is dashed with large components.

We can see the lagging line headed upwards and it has crossed the base line (not that that's relevant) but it is still firmly below the cloud itself. If we see the lagging line staying below the cloud while a bullish signal is generated, this means our signal is not as strong as it can be. The lagging line in this way adds an additional layer of confirmation to our entry and as we can see, is used to avoid entries which might not have the best odds of succeeding.

To clarify any confusions you might have, the chart I've shown above is historical. Therefore we will see the lagging line continuing all the way to the right edge of it. When trading live though, remember, the lagging line is 26 periods behind. Therefore it will end at the bar that is 26 bars behind the latest one. You need to see if the lagging line is above, below or within the cloud at that point which is 26 bars behind. This is a source of confusion amongst traders who being using this system so make sure you understand this point.

All in all the Ichimoku cloud gives us invaluable insight into predicting the movements of a stock. By using this, instead of purchasing the stock itself, you instead purchase a call in case of a long signal and a put in case of a bearish signal. Which strike price do you select? Well, my recommendation is to purchase the call with the strike price at your intended reward level. This is the same as having a take profit order at that level.

Next let us take a look at another indicator which helps us immensely.

Chapter 5: Buying Calls and Puts- Part 2

The Force Index particular oscillator relies on volume and is most effective in the stock markets or any market where volume data can be relied upon. Therefore, this indicator isn't very effective in FX markets because those do not have a centralized order book. Nonetheless, the Force Index is an extremely useful indicator both by itself and when combined with a trend measuring indicator. Developed by Dr. Alexander Elder and introduced in his book, Trading for a Living, the Force Index aims to measure the power of the bulls behind an uptrend and that of the bears behind every downtrend.

The philosophy of this indicator is simple. There are three essential elements to any movement of a stock: Extent, or length of the move, direction of price change and volume. These three elements are combined to form an oscillator which fluctuates between positive and negative territory. The originally stated use of this indicator was to determine the direction of the overall trend, forecast reversals via divergences and identify corrections in the trend which can enable us to get on board with the trend. While not all of these strategies work these days due to this indicator being extensively used, there are many other ways in which you can use this oscillator and it is worth studying this and adding it to your trading toolbox.

Visually, the force index is represented as fluctuating above and below zero. It is above zero when the bulls are in control and below when the bears are in control. The calculation of the force index involves calculating two components named the Force (1) and Force (13). In other words, the force index for 1 period and the 13 period force index. The calculation is as follows:

Force(1)= (Current close- prior close)* volume

Force(13)= 13 period EMA of Force (1)

The volume influences the values of the force index as is obvious to see. A large move on small volume will result in a small value for the indicator whereas a larger volume will give higher values. A positive value is obtained when the current close is above the previous one and negative when the current close is lesser than the previous bar. The raw value of the oscillator is plotted as a histogram with the center line as zero. The values are then plotted on the positive or negative side as appropriate and the curve is smoothed by using an EMA (I've used 13 in the calculation above). Technically you can use even a 2 day EMA but for practical purposes, a value above 10 is ideal.

When there is little volume or price movement, the indicator will hover around zero indicating low momentum currently present. Therefore in small ranges, one often sees such values printing. Needless to say, you want to avoid using this indicator or indeed trading when price is in a range. As explained in my other books, the best way to trade a range is to buy the lows and sell the highs. Only novices try to trade the middle and end up losing money as a result. Another point of importance that needs to be highlighted is that most traders, especially those trading the stock market, tend to fall in to the trap of trying to determine the perfect value for the number of EMA periods this indicator requires. I urge you to recognize the folly of this method of thinking and to fix your mindset and expectations with regards to trading and the process of doing so successfully. The correct way to approach this is to play around with the values and find one that is "good enough" as opposed to perfect. Perfection does exist in the markets but not in the way you think. I'll cover all of this in my book on trading mindset but for now just remember to avoid this trap.

The interpretation of the oscillator is quite straight forward. A positive value implies buyers were stronger than sellers and a negative one implies the opposite, that is, sellers stronger than buyers. The extent of price change gives us the distance price moved and can be seen as a proxy for the strength of buying or selling behind the move. Either way a large change between closing prices is something of note and this indicator perfectly captures it. The volume is a direct representation of the commitment, as Elder put it, of the players behind the move. A big move on a small volume is less reliable than a big move with a large number of players behind it. Those of you who are familiar with volume spread analysis will recognize the principle in play here. (For a discussion of the VSA strategy refer to my book Day Trading: Trade the Stock Market Like a Pro). The Force index manages to quantify all these elements into one chart and reading.

One of the uses of this indicator is to determine long term trend. A shorter time period will produce a more jagged, volatile curve whereas a lot of smoothing will occur over a larger time period. Traders most often use a 100 day period for the force index to determine long term trend changes and patterns. A crossover from below, that is from negative to positive, indicates a change from bearish to bullish and a crossover from above indicates a trend change to bearish from bullish. Once again, this is applicable only for longer time periods and on higher time frames. It doesn't make sense to try and spot long term trend characteristics on the 15 minute chart while using a look back period of 20. General advice is to use a 100 period look back period and the daily chart and above for this case.

The force index is most useful when day trading in my personal experience. When combined with some form of trend identification, a short term force index reading can be used to enter in the trend direction and take advantage of the end of small corrections. What I mean is, in an uptrend, for example, when a pullback occurs, a short term force index indicator will dip below zero due to its sensitivity. When it crosses back up above zero is when you enter in the trend direction. You can use an indicator that measure trend strength or direction like the ADX, Bollinger bands or EMAs or you can visually look at the trend. Another method is to use a higher period force index on the higher time frame and then trade the lower one with the lower look back period. Generally, I'd advise you to use a different indicator since its best to gather confirmation from multiple sources before trade entry. Traders can modulate the number of entries and activity level this strategy will produce by playing with the look back period on the indicator. Again, its essential to find a period which suits you the best, given your risk tolerance and cognitive loading abilities, as opposed to trying to find something that works "all the time" in the market. Practice using different values and go with the one that feels the easiest and makes you the most money on paper. For this strategy, do not trade counter trend and aim for a profit target of at least 2R or exit when the oscillator crosses over to the other side of the zero line, which ever comes first. So in a long position, you take your reward at either 2R (or you buy the call with a strike price at your intended level) or when the force index crosses into negative territory.

Another interesting way to use this indicator is to take advantage of its extreme readings. Now, ideally this strategy should not produce signals with great frequency, perhaps once a day if you're day trading, and generally I'd advise you to stay away from volatile stocks and instruments if you're using this strategy. The reason this strategy is effective is because of the volume component present in its calculation. When a stock or instrument experiences a volume spike, no matter the price direction, the value of the force index shoots up to an extreme value. Usually we'll see this then oscillate back down to more normal levels until the indicator reaches its prior low or high levels. The entry signal is when the indicator bounces up or down from the prior low or high. We enter on the close of that price bar and ride it for at least a 2R profit. While I appreciate this strategy is a bit difficult to understand in words, the charts at the end of this chapter will illustrate this method perfectly.

Like all other oscillators, the force index exhibits divergences from price. Unlike other oscillators though, I would caution you against trading a divergence. The divergence strategy is something which was first proposed by Elder in his book and many traders have since jumped on the band wagon and the strategy has been played to death. While I wouldn't advocate fading a divergence since that would be too risky, I would stay away from trading one since there's too much noise involved with every trader out there looking to get in on the action.

Combining the Force index with another oscillator works quite well but the best way of using this is to combine it with a trend indicator of some sort like the ADX or MACD. Again, its always better to have your entry signal confirmed by two separately derived indicators. There are some systems which choose to combine this with the RSI or Stochastic oscillator but I'm not keen on this since most of these systems are extremely mechanical and rely on a myriad of rules. Most traders will find that such systems work for a short while and then suddenly stop working because they were based on a quirk of the market which the system unearthed through pure luck. I'm mentioning this because you need to stay away from the temptation of thinking complex is better. The reality is the simpler your system is, the more successful you'll be. Limit yourself to two indicators at most and learn them inside out. It pays far more to use an indicator that suits you as opposed to making yourself fit a system.

The final strategy I'd like to highlight is one which requires a high risk tolerance and extreme mental discipline. Unlike most of the strategies I usually highlight, this is a counter trend approach and I would not recommend any beginner try this out. At the end of a trend, you'll often see the momentum flag and counter trend forces build up. The force index sometimes works as a leading indicator in such situations and you will see the indicator diverge from price. For example, you'll see price continue upwards while the force index either dips or goes flat. Now, this is the point where every single divergence trader get in and the effect is to usually push price in the trend direction even further because of the greater number of professional traders who fade this strategy. We meanwhile sit tight and watch the force index. They key characteristic to look for is to see whether the indicator retests the previous trend's trend line or support level. I do not mean trend line of the price or S/R level of price but the levels on the indicator itself. These prior levels are where momentum changes happened and its a good bet that the traders involved in making those changes there will be willing to participate again in the opposite direction. Thus as the force index retests those prior levels (on its own curve, NOT the price chart), we enter in a counter trend direction with a stop above or below a logical S/R level. As you can imagine, this involves you shorting or going long very near the top or bottom of the trend against it. This takes serious mental strength to do and requires a fair bit of training. This is why I do not recommend beginners trade this strategy, you'll simply burn yourself out.

The charts in the following pages will illustrate the various strategies we've looked at thus far.

The above chart illustrates a couple different methods by which you can trade the force index. The chart has a 20 EMA plotted on it. The instrument used is the FTSE 100 index. The interval I've used for the indicator is 13 and the time frame is 4 hour chart.

The force index is quite useful for determining trend reversals on any time frame. Here we see at the left of that chart a range which is at the end of a bear trend (not seen). Price stays in this range for a while and I've marked a long entry, indicated by the first vertical line with the arrow beneath it). At this point, we see the force index crossing the 0 level from below into positive territory. The EMA slope is flat. Similarly, the next vertical line also shows a similar logic behind the long entry. Flat EMA but force index crossing past 0 into positive territory. This is an example of a very aggressive way to trade this indicator. Here's my thought process behind this: Price is in a range and I'm reasoning that this range can be a good area for reversal. (Generally a large range following a trend indicates reversal. Please note: the range needs to be large relative to the preceding trend, you cannot blindly apply this to any old range as you please). Since I'm already on the lookout for a reversal, my strategy is to look for a low risk entry and get in on the bull trend as early as possible. This area is low risk since its so close to the bottom anyway while the potential reward is huge since it could result in a bull trend. With this thought process in mind, I decide to become aggressive and trade any bullish indication with my stop below the range bottom. At the first vertical line, I see a strong close above the EMA with the indicator crossing into positive territory. Given my aggressive outlook, I decide to enter despite the EMA staying flat. The second vertical line gives me an even better entry and at this point I just need to wait and watch. If the bull trend doesn't materialize, no matter, my risk is quite small. If it works out, I'll be making a significant amount of profit. As it turns out, it did work out and I'm now on board a nice bull trend from the start.

The rectangle marked in the middle of the chart is a place where most novice traders will get caught out. Either they blindly apply the previously mentioned aggressive approach of they see that the EMA has a slightly downward slope compared to previously and that the indicator has dipped below 0. They'll usually consider this a good place to go short and end up with a loss. The next logical step for them is to blame the indicator for not being good enough. The truth is such traders do not understand that you need to modulate your aggressiveness when entering the market. In this particular situation, we're in the first correction in a bull trend which has just started. This is the last place we want to be going short! So a dip below zero is an insignificant occurrence. If anything we ought to be waiting for the moment the indicator re-crosses the zero level into positive territory so we can get on board the bull trend. This is what the third vertical line is.

Note here that the entry criterion is a bit different from before. The trend is already established and the first correction has already taken place. Technically, the price could correct back a long way and we could still be in a bull trend. Therefore, my risk of entry here is a bit higher than previously. Therefore, I need a greater number of factors lining up in my favor. This is why, in addition to the positive cross over of the force index, I also look at the slope of the EMA (which is definitely tilting upwards) to make an entry decision. Remember, for the first 2 entries, I didn't consider the EMA slope and decided a strong close above it was good enough. This is because the risk involved at these positions is completely different, not to mention, the reward at this point is lesser than what was on offer at the previous levels simply due to the fact that there previous positions were entered before the trend had even begun.

As you can see, if you apply a little discretion to your trade entry decision, the rewards on offer are far more than a mechanical system. Trading a simple zero crossover system might have got you more entries and a small profit but by taking a step back and assessing the risk reward behind each position, we've made many multiples of profit compared to the mechanical system. This is how a professional thinks and you need to think this way as well if you wish to make big money in the markets. This doesn't mean you don't follow mechanical systems. Just understand their limitations. The flip side is that its easier to get started with a mechanical system than this discretionary method which requires you to do a lot of mental work. You really need to understand risk management and mindset principles to make this work. My recommendation would be to get started with a mechanical system, just pick one of the many I've listed in my other books and simultaneously work on the risk and mindset side of trading. This way, you'll make some money and when you're ready you can level up, so to speak, easily. In my opinion this is the best way to progress.

The daily chart of the FTSE shows how the force index can be used to determine long term trend changes. A prolonged range after a bear trend indicates change is afoot. The timing can be nailed down thanks to this indicator.

The force index decisively pops above 0 into positive territory right around the time the price starts making higher lows. Before the FTSE breaks out of the range, we've already established that accumulation has taken place and we're in a bull trend which will likely last a while.

The period used here for the force index is 100 as discussed previously. Notice how much smoother this line is around the 0 level and relative lack of crossovers.

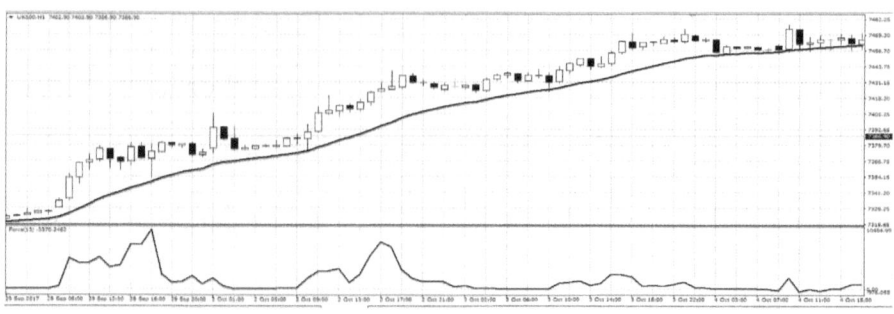

The most effective way to use this indicator is to day trade with it. The chart on top is the hourly chart showing a clear uptrend which we discern via the ema slope. Dropping down to the 15 minute chart of the FTSE, we see multiple moments when the force index crosses zero into positive territory enabling us to spot the end of the pullback and get on board the bull trend. The cross overs are highlighted by circles and the entry points are indicated by the rectangles.

The key is to spot the trend on the higher time frame correctly. You can use an indicator like the ADX for greater accuracy.

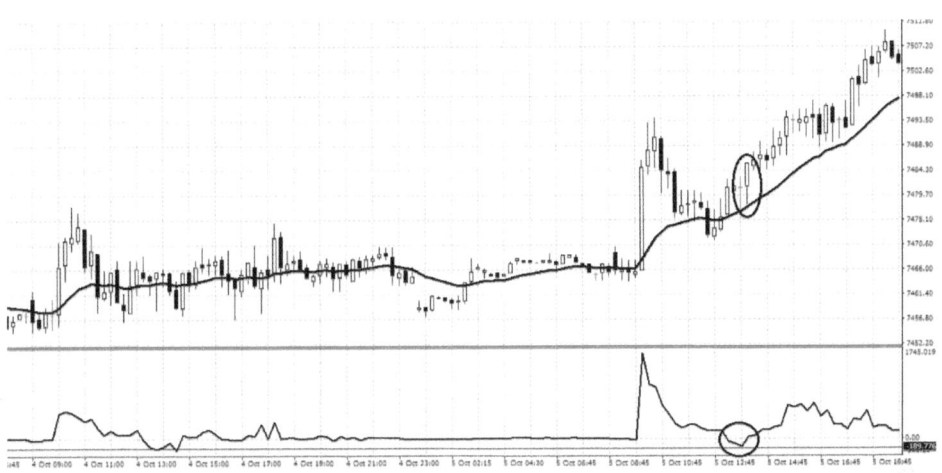

The circles illustrate how to use the force index when an extreme value is registered due to a volume spike. Notice how the indicator works its way back to a previous support level (in the indicator window look at the horizontal line).

Once the indicator bounces up from this line, we enter long (since the move that produced the spike was a bullish bar. Another method is to look at the EMA position vis-a-vis the price bar. In this case the bar is above the EMA and the EMA has a positive slope, all signs of bullishness).

This was on a 15 minute time frame. You won't see many signals like this but when it does occur. Its fairly easy to spot and trade.

An unconventional way of using the force index. Near the end of a bull trend, we see a trend line form on the oscillator. As price moves higher, the indicator forms a lower high which retests the flip side of the trend line. Seeing this, we short the subsequent bar with a stop some distance above based on higher time frame S/R principles.

This is not a strategy you will see present itself very often but it is lucrative when it does so. You will of course need extreme discipline to trade this and I do not recommend beginner traders trade this way.

Thus by using these 2 indicators, the force index and the ichimoku cloud, you can adapt a stocks trading strategy to your options trading and turbo charge your returns simply because due to the lower margin requirements, you can take more positions.

Now having looked at these very basic strategies, let's take it up a notch. Let's now look at 2 options strategies where the options behave as another leg of the trade and require more complexity for them to work.

Chapter 6: Option Strategy #1

The very reason traders choose options is due to their ability to limit the downside risk on any trade. Using options, not only can we limit the downside of a trade but we can also ensure we get paid while holding on to the position. This is the basis of the strategies we'll be looking at. Again, if you're not yet comfortable with risk profiles, I suggest you go back and practice them thoroughly until you are. The mechanics of these strategies will not make sense unless you do.

The first strategy we'll be looking at is a synthetic call strategy. Now this isn't a strategy that relies on options alone but is one where the option part of the strategy limits your downside by a huge margin. Such strategies are perfect for transitioning from trading stocks to options since they effectively form a bridge between both styles. As such this is the transition I recommend to anyone getting started with trading options. The synthetic call essentially works to reduce your maximum possible loss to the price of the option involved as opposed to a theoretical possibility of the stock going all the way to 0. The strategy will make more sense when viewed using the following numbers.

Let's say we purchase a share of AAPL for 25$. Even if we do have a stop loss at 23, there's no guarantee the market will hit that price. There could be a major event and the price could go all the way back down to 0. Hence our maximum risk on this trade is 25. How do we reduce this risk?

Well, we buy a put on AAPL with a strike price at the level where we're willing to stomach a maximum loss. In other words, the closer to the entry level you buy the put, the lesser your maximum loss will be. If you purchase a put with a strike price of 25, then your loss is limited to the cost of the put. If you buy the put at a strike price of 23, then you will lose 2$ plus the cost of the put. Visualize it via the scenario below:

Stock purchased at 25$

Put strike price= 25$

Cost of put= 5$ (assumed value)

Now if the stock price goes all the way to 0 upon option expiry then:

Loss on stock purchase= 0-25 (sell price- buy price)= -25$

Profit on put position= 25-0-5 (sell-buy- cost of put option)=

20$

Total P/L= -25+20= -5$

If the stock price goes to 50$ upon option expiry then:

Profit on stock purchase= 50-25= 25$

Loss on put position= -5 (cost of option which is now worthless)

Total P/L= 25-5= 20$

Break even point for position= 25+5= 30 (purchase price+ cost of put)

This gives us the risk profile as below:

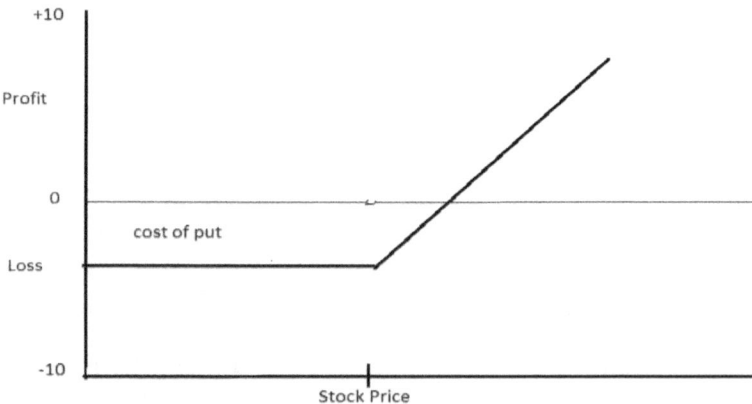

You will notice that this risk profile is very similar to that of a call, that is buying a call at the strike price of 25 without purchasing the underlying stock if you think the stock is going to rise. While the risk profile is the same, the numbers involved are slightly different. The 2 strategies are not fully interchangeable and should be chosen on the basis of your risk profile. Let's look at the numbers and compare the two approaches using the same numbers are previously.

Cost of synthetic call= cost of stock+cost of put= 25+5= 30$

Risk= maximum loss= cost of put= 5$

Break even= 25+5= 30$

Reward= unlimited

Cost of long call= 5$ (strike price of 25. Assuming the same price as the put for simplicity).

Risk= maximum loss= cost of call= 5$

Break even= 25+5= 30$

Reward= unlimited

Comparing the 2 we can see they have the same break even price. Now this is the case only in this example. In reality, the put will be price slightly cheaper than the call so in the real world, the break even of the synthetic call will be slightly lower than of the long call. The next thing that really stands out is the comparative costs. The synthetic call costs us 30$ but the long call comes in at a cheap 5$. The risk is comparable as well. So what's the upside with the synthetic call then? Well, the upside exactly illustrates the difference in the thinking between an amateur and professional trader. Professionals think in terms of risk. Amateurs think in terms of cost and reward.

The risk of the synthetic call is a mere 16% of the cost of the position. We get this number by dividing the maximum loss by the total cost, in this case, that would be 5/30. In the case of the long call, this value would be 100%. This has huge implications for your trading. With the risk so drastically lowered, you can actually take a far larger position in the market with the synthetic call as opposed to the long call while still sticking to your overall risk parameters. In other words, you'll be risking the same percentage of your capital with the two strategies but be able to take a position roughly double the size with the first strategy.

Thus, if the trade moves in your favor, you're making a far larger amount than someone who simply buys the call at 25.

As you can see, by simply purchasing a put, we've actually improved drastically a simple long strategy that most traders use. So if your trading system gives you a long signal, go ahead and place a trade and your stop. But also purchase a put with the strike price either equal to the entry price. This way, you can take larger positions and make many multiples of what you'd have usually made. A word of warning though. This works only if your stop loss is at least equal in distance from your entry as the cost of the put. Let's see an example of this:

<u>Example 1</u>

Entry price=25$

SL=23$

Cost of put= 5$ (strike price of 25)

If price hits the SL of 23

Total loss on the stock position= -2$ (sold at 23- bought at 25)

Total profit on the put= 2-5= -3$ (bought at 23- sold at 25- cost of put)

Total p/L= -2-3= -5$ (the cost of the option in other words)

Example 2

Entry price= 25$

SL= 20$

Cost of put=5$ (strike price of 25)

If price hits the SL of 20

Total loss on the stock position= -5$

Total profit on the put= 5-5=0 (bought at 20- sold at 25- cost of put)

Total P/L= -5$ (cost of option which is the same as the SL distance).

Example 3

Entry price= 25$

SL= 15$

Cost of put=5$ (strike price of 25)

If price hits the SL of 20

Total loss on the stock position=-10$

Total profit on the put= 10-5=5 (bought at 15- sold at 25- cost of put)

Total P/L= -5$ (cost of option)

Let's dissect example 3 further in terms of position sizing. If you had purchased the stock as usual as per your strategy you would have been risking 10 points (per share). If you had a 5000$ account and were risking 2% per trade, your total risk amount is 100$. At 10$ per point this gives you a maximum position size of 10 shares. Assuming you bought the put, your maximum possible risk has been reduced to 5$. So your maximum position size while risking 2% of your account is now 20 shares despite keeping the same stop loss distance. Let's look at a profit scenario:

Purchase price= 25$

Selling price= 50$

Cost of put@strike 25= 5$

Profit on stock sale= 50-25= 25$

Loss on put= 5$

Profit amount assuming only stock purchase= 10*25= 250$ (position of 10 shares)

Profit amount assuming synthetic call strategy= 20*25= 500-5= 495$ (position of 20 shares)

The stock only scenario yields a profit of 5% while the synthetic call yields a whopping 9.9% profit. Despite having the same stop loss as your original strategy! I hope the power of the synthetic call is clear to you now. Also from the preceding example you can see why its crucial that your put is price lower than your stop loss distance in points. For those of you trading forex, you'll need to work out your cost per pip and multiply it with the number of pips to your stop loss and then compare it to the price of the put.

I've of course used plain vanilla numbers in the examples above. Despite the numbers being different in real life though, the principle remains the same. Run the numbers based on whatever prices you get and if it makes sense, pull the trigger on the synthetic call strategy. A simple way to think of this strategy is that by purchasing a put, you're purchasing insurance on your position. The larger the premium you pay, the lower your risk. The flip side is the larger the premium, the farther away your break even point is. Don't get too bogged down trying to figure out the perfect price to purchase the put. This is a mistake all beginners make. Remember that its all about the math with this strategy and as long as it works, go ahead and pull the trigger.

Ideally, you'll want to purchase the put at your entry point but if the math works out, purchasing a put slightly above stop loss level works just as well. The put near your stop loss level will be priced lower compared to the put at your entry point so you can take a larger position size by buying there. Before you run away with yourself though, remember to not go beyond your stop loss to purchase your put. If you do not completely understand that sentence, go back and review the examples and work them out step by step. Options trading requires you to make adjustments from trading in a purely visual way so its always s bit steep in the beginning.

Now that we've covered synthetic calls, lets look at another popular beginner strategy: the covered call.

Chapter 7: Option Strategy #2

The next strategy we're looking at will give us more flexibility when we go long on a stock. This strategy, called the covered call, effectively mixes the best of worlds by giving us a long position on a stock and also gives us some income while we hold on to the position. Comparing this with a regular long strategy and you can see why this is a great improvement and its all thanks to the option part of the strategy.

The way the covered call strategy works is this: You go long a stock as per your trading system. Once this is done, you sell a call option with a strike price that is at least 2 levels out of the money with an expiration date a month away. Now, I know I've only mentioned buying options thus far so this is a new complexity I'm introducing here.

When you sell an option, you're obligated to either buy or sell the underlying stock if it happens to be in the money up on expiration. For example if you sell a call option for AAPL with a strike price of 25$ expiring one month from now. In one month's time, if the stock price is 26$, you are obligated to sell shares of apple to the option buyer. Remember the option buyer can choose to exercise the option upon expiry and in the case of a call this gives them the right to buy the underlying stock. As a seller of a call option, you must sell them the stock they intend to buy. Similarly, in the case of selling a put, which gives the buyer of the put the right to sell the underlying stock, you are obligated to buy the stock from the purchaser of the put if the option is in the money up on expiration. If the option happens to be out of the money up on expiry, that is below the strike price for a call and above th strike price for a put, then you get to pocket the option premium.

In the case of selling options, as you can see, your profit is capped at the option premium but your loss is far greater. What do you think the risk profile of a call sell and a put sell will be? Compare it to the figures below and see how well you understand this.

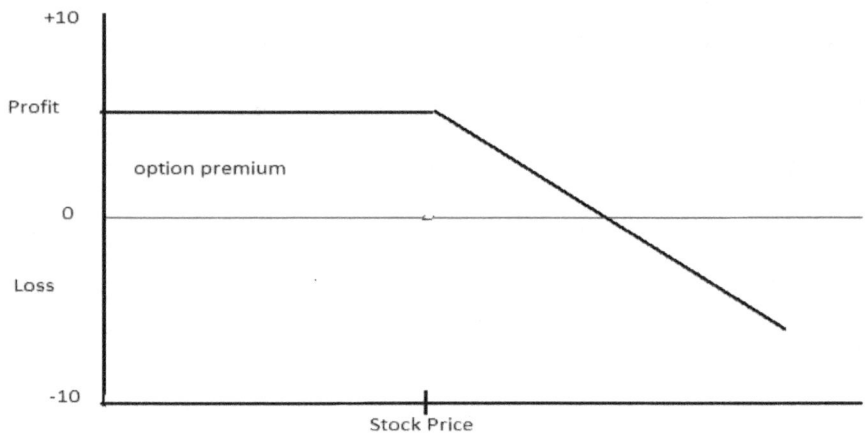

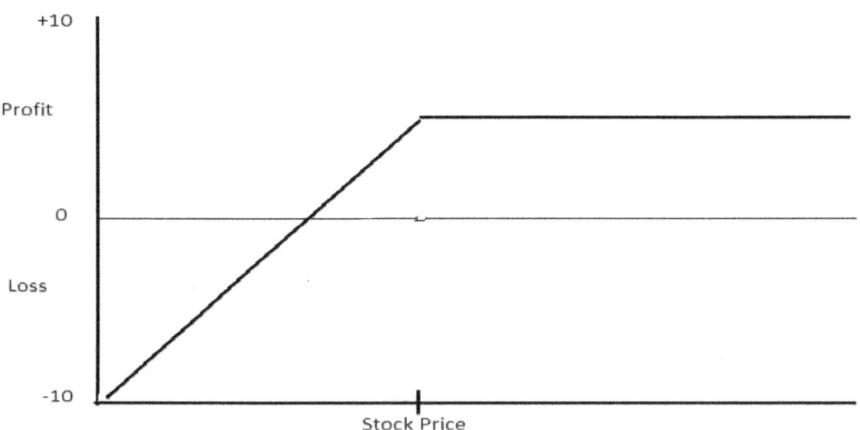

Generally when you buy an option, the idea is to give yourself as much time as possible to let it play out. After all, you want the trade to give as much room to breathe right? The opposite is true when selling an option. You want as little time left as possible to the expiry date since a longer time line exposes you to greater risk. Simply put, there a greater number of things that can happen the longer you're in the trade, that is, the option's expiry date is longer. This is great if you're long an option and bad if you're short.

Another reason for wanting short term options is that their prices are always higher than that of longer term options. I'm speaking of in the money or at the money options here. Options which are way out of the money will have no value beyond the time value but those even a bit out of the money will have a greater cost than those further away. This way your profits are larger when your expiry date is closer. Selling options is an extremely risky strategy and should only be done when you're experienced enough. Some broker will not even allow you to sell calls due to the unlimited risk they pose since there is no upward limit to a price rise.

In a covered call though, selling an option is acceptable because you're doing it as part of a strategy and not doing it naked. The way it works is this: let's say you're long AAPL at 25$ and you sell the call with a strike price of 30$ at a premium of 0.8$ (80 cents). Remember the price needs to be higher than 30$ for us to take a loss on the call portion of this trade. Let's work out our scenarios again like previously upon expiry:

Scenario 1: Price is 0

Loss on stock trade= 0-25=-25

Profit on option= 0.8 (since the call is worthless, we keep the premium the buyer paid us)

Total P/L= -25+0.8= -24.20 $

Scenario 2: Price is 22

Loss on stock trade= 22-25=-3

Profit on option trade= 0.8

Total P/L= -3+.8= -3.20$

Scenario 3: Price is 24.20$

Loss on stock trade= 24.2-25= -0.80

Profit on option trade= 0.8

Total P/L= -0.8+0.8=0

Scenario 4: Price is 25 (same as purchase price)

Loss on stock trade= 25-25=0

Profit on option trade= 0.8

Total P/L= 0+0.8= 0.80

Scenario 5: Price is 30

Gain on stock trade= 30-25=5

Loss on option trade= option premium paid by buyer to us+Strike price-current price upon option exercise by buyer= 0.8+30-30= 0.80

Total P/L= 5+0.8= 5.80

Scenario 6: Price is 35

Gain on stock trade= 35-25=10

Loss on option trade= 0.8+30-35= -4.20

Total P/L= 10-4.2= 5.80

Scenario 7: Price is 50

Gain on stock trade= 50-25=25

Loss on option trade= 0.8+30-50=-19.20

Total P/L= 25-19.2= 5.80

As you can see, our maximum profit is capped at an amount equal to (strike price- buy price)+option premium. While this may seem a bit nonsensical, especially consider the previous chapter where we were able to limit our downside potential and greatly expand our profit potential, you must realize a few things. First off all, a majority of options expire out of the money and thus this is a great way to collect a dividend while holding on to a long position. A second thing to consider is that if you are bullish on a stock but not much so, the covered call is a method of profiting on both the long stock call as well as the option side.

The question when executing a covered call strategy is at what price should you sell the call at? Well, let's look at the previous example and work our way through it. Let's say we sell a call that is in the money at 25 instead of 30 and the option is priced at 3$ (assuming no time value for simplicity).

Scenario 1: Price is 0

Loss on stock trade= 0-25=-25

Profit on option= 3 (since the call is worthless, we keep the premium the buyer paid us)

Total P/L= -25+3= -22 $

Scenario 2: Price is 22

Loss on stock trade= 22-25=-3

Profit on option trade= 3

Total P/L= -3+3= 0$/break even

Scenario 3: Price is 24$

Loss on stock trade= 24-25= -1

Loss on option trade= option premium paid by buyer to us+Strike price-current price upon option exercise by buyer= 3+22-24=1

Total P/L= -1+1=0/ break even

Scenario 4: Price is 25 (same as purchase price)

Loss on stock trade= 25-25=0

Loss on option trade= 3+22-25=0

Total P/L= 0+0= break even

Scenario 5: Price is 30

Gain on stock trade= 30-25=5

Loss on option trade= 3+22-30= -4

Total P/L= 5-4= 1

Scenario 6: Price is 35

Gain on stock trade= 35-25=10

Loss on option trade= 3+22-35= -10

Total P/L= 10-10= 0

Scenario 7: Price is 50

Gain on stock trade= 50-25=25

Loss on option trade= 3+22-50=-25

Total P/L= 25-25= 0

As you can see selling an in the money call gives you more scenarios where you're likely to break even and to avoid a loss. The flip side is that you won't make much money either. As a beginner, I recommend you play around with the scenarios such as those described above and understand the relationship between the call premium and prices and your bottom line. In these examples I've ignored the time value of the option to make it simpler to understand. In reality you'll find that some scenarios will give you a loss equal to your time value. Ultimately it comes down to what price you're willing to pay and how much risk you wish to stomach.

The covered call gives us a risk profile exactly like that of selling a naked put, that is selling a put option and only the option. Much like how we saw on the synthetic call though, there are differences, mostly in terms of risk. Consider the scenario below.

Using the same example as previously:

- Buy the stock at 25 and sell the 30 call for 0.50.
- Sell the 20 put for 0.50

Total cost of covered call= 25-0.5= 24.50

Risk= 25-0.5= 24.50.

Maximum reward= call premium received+strike price- cost price= 0.5+30-25=5.50

Break even= 25-0.5=24.5 i.e cost price- option premium received.

Total cost of naked put= 0/ You will receive the put premium

Risk= 20-0.5= 19.5

Maximum reward= 0.5/ limited to the put premium received.

Break even= 20-0.5= 19.50

Let's break down the risk characteristics. In the case of the covered call ,your risk is 100% of your investment. In the case of the put, you don't have any cost but your risk is many many multiples greater than your maximum reward. Your maximum risk to reward ratio in the case of the covered call is 22.4% while in the case of the naked put it is a 2.5%. The thing to consider here though is that aside from requiring margin funds in your account, you do not need to put any funds down for selling the put. This does give you advantages but the flip side is your reward is duly limited. The covered call gives you a greater return but costs a lot more.

Ultimately, like we saw in the previous chapter, a lot depends on your risk profile and how much you wish to spend on the trade.

The covered call does have an impediment in that the maximum risk is rather huge. The best way to mitigate this would be to run this strategy on stocks which are trending upwards in a non volatile manner. However, such stocks will have a low premium and this pushes most traders to go and mess with the stocks that are more volatile. Now, if you know what you're doing, playing with a volatile stock can be profitable. As a beginner however, I urge you to resist the greed and stick to earning regular and decent premiums.

An advanced strategy called a collar can be used to mitigate risk. The collar essentially simulates the best of both worlds by capping your downside risk and the upside. Such a strategy is beyond the scope of this book but can be found in any book on advanced options strategies.

Chapter 8: Putting it All Together

In this book we started off by looking at what options are, how to evaluate brokers, how to adapt a stock trading strategy to an option template and finally 2 strategies you can use by employing options as another leg of your trade.

There are many more strategies you can use with options but I recommend familiarizing yourself with the ones listed thus far. Once you've done this, then move on to more complex strategies. Take my word for it, you will not be able to successfully execute an advanced strategy unless you have mastered the basics I've listed here first.

I hope you found this book useful and hopefully it wasn't overwhelming. I've done my best to explain things in as simple a manner as possible. If you feel you liked this book and it was of use to you, please do leave a review on amazon. Also, do check out my other books on trading. As someone with extensive experience I'm positive I can assist you in many ways.

I wish you the best of luck in your journey in trading!

www.ingramcontent.com/pod-product-compliance
Lightning Source LLC
Chambersburg PA
CBHW020453220526
45464CB00002B/971